Dedication

To my beautiful children, Amari and Harper.

Amari, you've witnessed some of my struggles and I'm sorry for that. Your unwavering love has helped in my healing process. Thank you for being patient with me.
Now you'll receive the best of me.

Harper, mommy had to grow in order to bring you into the world and raise you as a healthy woman to be. I'm excited for this journey.

Together we will be love and light.

Welcome!

You're here because it's time for you to let go of the life that you once knew in order to gain the one that you deserve.

When we think of self-care, we mostly think of tangible things: Mani-pedi, clean house, bubble baths, etc. Even though these things can help us feel good, it's all momentary and often leaves you searching for more.

In this workbook, you're going to learn to set your intentions so that self-care for the mind is always at the top of your to-do list.

Check-In. Show Up. Be Love.

I then buried it all and moved forward.

My world is so different now. I'm unafraid of letting go, setting healthy boundaries and enjoying life how I choose.

The power of knowing oneself makes a huge difference in how life is lived. I prioritize differently now. I'm first because if I don't show up for myself to protect and love, I can't expect others to want to do the same.

I love freely with no guards and make time to check in with myself, meditate and maintain a balanced life.

I'm glad to say that I am happy!

Check In

A Simple Guide to Self-Care

The guided self-improvement journal that'll empower you to become a healthier version: mentally, physically and spiritually.

Great change happens when you're consistent so stay the course to witness your greatness.

The content in this book is not intended to replace therapy or any medical grade advice. This is strictly based on personal experiences and research. Therapy is a good tool for healing and isn't just for those with diagnosed mental instabilities, so please don't be afraid to seek the help that you need.

In order for this content to work for you, you have to be ready to accept who you are and your placement in life, take accountability, stay consistent and do the necessary work to grow.

You will learn to free yourself from: self-sabotaging, impostor syndrome and shame.
You will accomplish: understanding purpose, focus, forgiveness, healing, grief and wholeness.

One thing that can stunt your growth mentally, spiritually, and physically is the inability to accept yourself for who you really are.

If have lived a little bit of life, you're going to have shortcomings. There's no need to glamorize your truth for the likes of others. That is like a gateway drug that can eventually spiral into the normalization of dysfunction.

There is no quick scheme or trick that leads to happiness or wholeness.
It's not found in things or people; that's all temporary satisfaction.
The work starts within, and this guide will assist you.
I will not pretend that this process is soft or that it will make you feel good. It's healing and growth — sometimes that's painful.
 If you've ever told a lie and was caught, you may feel like a fraud in that moment. You may also have these same feelings when you're forced to be honest with yourself about some hard truths. Allow yourself grace; You're learning.

HEAL
From brokenness, betrayal, trauma and insecurities.
Heal: to become healthy.

Healing is the process of curing wounds and brokenness.
Healing comes in waves. You may feel great one day and think that something is out of your system, but find yourself breaking into tears about that thing on another day.
The goal of healing isn't to just get over something, the goal is to move forward with a healthy mindset, peace and understanding.
You can't undo trauma overnight, so be patient and allow yourself grace. When you're consistent with the process, your days will become easier.

GROW
From immaturity, shame, stagnancy, and unhealthy mindsets.
Grow: to progress onward.
Growth is the process of acceptance, letting go, and moving forward.
We all get older, but we don't always grow.

You can live a whole life with people and things constantly changing around you, but if you make no efforts, you'll just live one long day. This happens when you settle and become comfortable doing the same things and being the same person day to day. If you never change, you'll never grow.

GLOW

From a healthy mindset and lifestyle: mentally, physically, and spiritually

Glow: to shine from within.

Glowing is the process of living a purposeful life—equal to a happy life.

Once you decide to heal and grow, the next step is to live a balanced life. Having balance makes a difference in how you approach everything. Your focus shifts, dysfunctional behaviors become uncomfortable, bad days becomes momentary.

Write your own:

Personal Mission Statement:

A mission statement helps to determine your values by sharing your ultimate goal and how you'll accomplish them.

Set concrete goals, be honest about the things that you need to complete, make a list and check them off accordingly.

_____
_____
_____
_____

Short-term goals: these can be daily, weekly, or annually.

What is your short-term goal, and what do you plan to do to accomplish this goal?

_____
_____
_____
_____

Long-term goals: Something to accomplish In the future.

The amount of time is determined by you but make sure they're realistic and that your short-term goals are helping you achieve long-term goals.

_____
_____

_____

_____

Example:

My mission statement: I will become a healthier version of myself mentally, physically, and spiritually so that I can help others do the same.

Long-term goal: In three years, I want to be a traveling yoga instructor with clientele in three states.

Short-term goal: I will practice yoga at least three times a week, meditate daily for at least ten mins, eat less junk food and more healthy meals that are made for my body, practice mindfulness and positivity.

My mission statement: Become a healthier version of myself mentally, physically, and spiritually so that I can help others do the same.

BE HONEST. THE ANSWERS ARE A TEST TO SEE HOW MUCH YOU'RE WILLING TO SHOW UP FOR YOURSELF.

Have you ever had a vision of a greater version of yourself living a better life?
1. Yes
2. No

Do you believe that the vision could become your reality?
1. Yes
2. No

If there is work to do to achieve this life, are you willing to work for it?

Through proper preparation, honesty, and follow-through, you can become the best version of yourself.
You're the only one who has full control of your life, and it is you that has to make the efforts to become better.

Accept your journey as if you're seeking a healthier lifestyle vs. taking on new tasks so that reaching your goals seems less like chores and more like accomplishments.

Stay the course, and you'll live a new life with greater opportunity, understanding, peace and love.

NOTE: In order to create healthy life habits, you must get rid of any bad ones.
Letting go of anything that you've normalized isn't "easy", but it is doable. Be kind to yourself in the process. You can only fail if you give up.

Name a bad habit that you should let go of.

_____

Will you let go of this habit?

_____

How can this improve your life?

_____

_____

_____

Let's start with a list of things that fuel you (excites you, makes you move) and a list of things that drain you.

It's ok if you can't think of anything or everything right now, you can always come back.

When you unlock your existing trauma and triggers, you'll understand the things that you need to let go of and what more to take in.

Fuels:

_____

_____

_____

Drains:

_____

_____

_____

What did you learn here?

_____

_____

_____

Make plans to do more of what fuels you and less of what drains you.

Begin each day anew by giving in to what you could learn or change.   (Do this daily) Write as much as you can for each task.

This will help you to become mindful and create a healthy daily routine.

Dream from the night before: What do you remember?

_____

_____

What do you think the dream meant?

_____

_____

Meditation: What did you learn or let go of?

_____

_____

Schedule: Write three tasks to complete starting with the most important one.

_____

_____

Personal Development: Will you make time for image & health? (Grooming—nails, feet, brows, hair, skincare, makeup etc.) If yes, which is your priority?

_____

Healthy meals - Eat something healthy today

Note:
Healthy means to promote good health—it doesn't mean salad only. Find something that you may enjoy while protecting your body from harm. A healthy gut can help with the healing of an unhealthy mind.

Note: Meal prep is a great option for those who are constantly on the go. If outsourcing is an option, try a meal prepping company.

_____

Exercise - 10-20 minutes a day of movement is better than zero minutes.

_____

Gratitude: What are three things you're grateful for?

_____
_____
_____

Quick Journal: Write one sentence or paragraph of true emotions for the day.

_____
_____
_____
_____

Meditation: Is there anything that you need to release or need clarity on?

_____
_____
_____

"Make time to love on yourself.
If you feel guilty for taking care of yourself, take a step back and remind yourself that if you're not whole; nothing else you touch will be."

Daily Food Tracker:

Food is essential for health, so please eat. If you have goals to change in any way, get a health exam first and speak with your doctor about any issues that you may have or notice.

Diets aren't created equally, so be mindful of trying them just because they're popular.

This tracker is a good way to get in tune with your body; learn how it acts and reacts to food and the missing nutrients.

Don't hold back on your truth. You're the only judge here.

Day 1:

Breakfast:
_____

Snack:
_____

Lunch:
_____

Snack:
_____

Dinner:
_____

Snack:
_____

Reminder: Be honest! If you woke up and had a warm donut and a cup of sugar with a splash of coffee, write it down.

Check In:

How did you feel once you'd eaten each item?

If you pay attention, your body will tell you when something is and isn't right for you.

_____

_____

Is there anything from today's list that you should get rid of or only eat in moderation?

_____

If so, what?

Are you ready to make these changes? Why or why not?

_____

_____

What did you enjoy the most of all meals?

_____

Instead of giving yourself time limits, give yourself time frames. It'll help you to stop placing limits on yourself and think more about the bigger picture.

The thing about clarity is that it'll lead you to the truth and sometimes that may be uncomfortable.
It's your truth, don't run from it.
Sit in it, accept it, learn from it and move forward.

QUALI J.

Gratitude: What are three things you're grateful for?

_____

_____

_____

Quick Journal: Write one sentence or paragraph of true emotions for the day.

_____

_____

_____

_____

_____

Meditation: Is there anything that you need to release or need clarity on?

_____

Daily Food Tracker:

Day 2:

Breakfast:
_____

Snack:
_____

Lunch:
_____

Snack:
_____

Dinner:

_____

Snack:
_____

Check In:

How did you feel once you'd eaten each item?

If you pay attention, your body will tell you when something is and isn't right for you.

_____

_____

Is there anything from today's list that you should get rid of or only eat in moderation?

_____

If so, what?

Are you ready to make these changes? Why or why not?

_____

_____

What did you enjoy the most of all meals?

_____

Instead of giving yourself time limits, give yourself time frames. It'll help you to stop placing limits on yourself and think more about the bigger picture.

Gratitude: What are three things you're grateful for?

_____

_____

_____

Quick Journal: Write one sentence or paragraph of true emotions for the day.

_____

_____

_____

_____

_____

Meditation: Is there anything that you need to release or need clarity on?

_____

Daily Food Tracker:

Day 3:

Breakfast:
_____

Snack:
_____

Lunch:
_____

Snack:
_____

Dinner:
_____

Snack:

Check In:

How did you feel once you'd eaten each item?

If you pay attention, your body will tell you when something is and isn't right for you.

_____

_____

Is there anything from today's list that you should get rid of or only eat in moderation?

_____

If so, what?

Are you ready to make these changes? Why or why not?

_____

_____

What did you enjoy the most of all meals?

_____

Instead of giving yourself time limits, give yourself time frames. It'll help you to stop placing limits on yourself and think more about the bigger picture.

Gratitude: What are three things you're grateful for?

_____
_____
_____

Quick Journal: Write one sentence or paragraph of true emotions for the day.

_____
_____
_____
_____

Meditation: Is there anything that you need to release or need clarity on?

_____

Daily Food Tracker:

Day 4:

Breakfast:
_____

Snack:
_____

Lunch:
_____

Snack:
_____

Dinner:
_____

Snack:

Be careful when comparing yourself to others. They may have something that you want, but you don't know what it took to get it and you don't know if you'd actually love it if you were to have it.

Check In:

How did you feel once you'd eaten each item?

If you pay attention, your body will tell you when something is and isn't right for you.

_____

_____

Is there anything from today's list that you should get rid of or only eat in moderation?

_____

If so, what?

Are you ready to make these changes? Why or why not?

_____

_____

What did you enjoy the most of all meals?

_____

Instead of giving yourself time limits, give yourself time frames. It'll help you to stop placing limits on yourself and think more about the bigger picture.

"When you're spiritually connected, you'll be shown things that could save you from the very things you're dodging."

Gratitude: What are three things you're grateful for?

_____

_____

_____

Quick Journal: Write one sentence or paragraph of true emotions for the day.

_____

_____

_____

_____

Meditation: Is there anything that you need to release or need clarity on?

_____

Daily Food Tracker:

Day 5:

Breakfast:

_____

Snack:

_____

Lunch:

_____

Snack:

_____

Dinner:

_____

Snack:

_____

Check In:

How did you feel once you'd eaten each item?

If you pay attention, your body will tell you when something is and isn't right for you.

_____

_____

Is there anything from today's list that you should get rid of or only eat in moderation?

_____

If so, what?

Are you ready to make these changes? Why or why not?

_____

_____

What did you enjoy the most of all meals?

_____

Instead of giving yourself time limits, give yourself time frames. It'll help you to stop placing limits on yourself and think more about the bigger picture.

Gratitude: What are three things you're grateful for?

_____

_____

_____

Quick Journal: Write one sentence or paragraph of true emotions for the day.

_____

_____

_____

_____

_____

Meditation: Is there anything that you need to release or need clarity on?

_____

Daily Food Tracker:

Day 6:

Breakfast:

_____

Snack:

_____

Lunch:

_____

Snack:

_____

Dinner:

_____

Snack:

Check In:

How did you feel once you'd eaten each item?

If you pay attention, your body will tell you when something is and isn't right for you.

_____

_____

Is there anything from today's list that you should get rid of or only eat in moderation?

_____

If so, what?

Are you ready to make these changes? Why or why not?

_____

_____

What did you enjoy the most of all meals?

_____

Instead of giving yourself time limits, give yourself time frames. It'll help you to stop placing limits on yourself and think more about the bigger picture.

Gratitude: What are three things you're grateful for?

_____

_____

_____

Quick Journal: Write one sentence or paragraph of true emotions for the day.

_____

_____

_____

_____

_____

Meditation: Is there anything that you need to release or need clarity on?

_____

Daily Food Tracker:

Day 7:

Breakfast:

_____

Snack:

_____

Lunch:

_____

Snack:

_____

Dinner:

_____

Snack:

_____

Check In:

How did you feel once you'd eaten each item?

If you pay attention, your body will tell you when something is and isn't right for you.

_____

_____

Is there anything from today's list that you should get rid of or only eat in moderation?

_____

If so, what?

Are you ready to make these changes? Why or why not?

_____

_____

What did you enjoy the most of all meals?

_____

Instead of giving yourself time limits, give yourself time frames. It'll help you to stop placing limits on yourself and think more about the bigger picture.

Gratitude: What are three things you're grateful for?

_____

_____

_____

Quick Journal: Write one sentence or paragraph of true emotions for the day.

_____

_____

_____

_____

Meditation: Is there anything that you need to release or need clarity on?

_____

Daily Food Tracker:

Day 8:

Breakfast:
_____

Snack:
_____

Lunch:
_____

Snack:
_____

Dinner:
_____

Snack:
_____

Check In:

How did you feel once you'd eaten each item?

If you pay attention, your body will tell you when something is and isn't right for you.

_____

_____

Is there anything from today's list that you should get rid of or only eat in moderation?

_____

If so, what?

Are you ready to make these changes? Why or why not?

_____

_____

What did you enjoy the most of all meals?

_____

Instead of giving yourself time limits, give yourself time frames. It'll help you to stop placing limits on yourself and think more about the bigger picture.

Gratitude: What are three things you're grateful for?

_____

_____

_____

Quick Journal: Write one sentence or paragraph of true emotions for the day.

_____
_____
_____
_____
_____

Meditation: Is there anything that you need to release or need clarity on?

_____

Daily Food Tracker:

Day 9

Breakfast:
_____

Snack:
_____

Lunch:
_____

Snack:
_____

Dinner:
_____

Snack:
_____

Check In:

How did you feel once you'd eaten each item?

If you pay attention, your body will tell you when something is and isn't right for you.

_____

_____

Is there anything from today's list that you should get rid of or only eat in moderation?

_____

If so, what?

Are you ready to make these changes? Why or why not?

_____

_____

What did you enjoy the most of all meals?

_____

Instead of giving yourself time limits, give yourself time frames. It'll help you to stop placing limits on yourself and think more about the bigger picture.

Gratitude: What are three things you're grateful for?

_____

_____

_____

Quick Journal: Write one sentence or paragraph of true emotions for the day.

_____

_____

_____

_____

Meditation: Is there anything that you need to release or need clarity on?

_____

Daily Food Tracker:

Day 10:

Breakfast:

_____

Snack:

_____

Lunch:

_____

Snack:

_____

Dinner:

_____

Snack:

_____

Check In:

How did you feel once you'd eaten each item?

If you pay attention, your body will tell you when something is and isn't right for you.

_____

_____

Is there anything from today's list that you should get rid of or only eat in moderation?

_____

If so, what?

Are you ready to make these changes? Why or why not?

_____

_____

What did you enjoy the most of all meals?

_____

Instead of giving yourself time limits, give yourself time frames. It'll help you to stop placing limits on yourself and think more about the bigger picture.

Gratitude: What are three things you're grateful for?

_____

_____

_____

Quick Journal: Write one sentence or paragraph of true emotions for the day.

_____

_____

_____

_____

Meditation: Is there anything that you need to release or need clarity on?

_____

Daily Food Tracker:

Day 11:

Breakfast:
_____

Snack:
_____

Lunch:
_____

Snack:
_____

Dinner:
_____

Snack:
_____

Check In:

How did you feel once you'd eaten each item?

If you pay attention, your body will tell you when something is and isn't right for you.

_____

_____

Is there anything from today's list that you should get rid of or only eat in moderation?

_____

If so, what?

Are you ready to make these changes? Why or why not?

_____

_____

What did you enjoy the most of all meals?

_____

Instead of giving yourself time limits, give yourself time frames. It'll help you to stop placing limits on yourself and think more about the bigger picture.

Gratitude: What are three things you're grateful for?

_____

_____

Quick Journal: Write one sentence or paragraph of true emotions for the day.

_____

_____

_____

_____

Meditation: Is there anything that you need to release or need clarity on?

_____

Daily Food Tracker:

Don't hold back on your truth. You're the only judge here.

Day 12:

Breakfast:

_____

Snack:

_____

Lunch:

_____

Snack:

_____

Dinner:

_____

Snack:

_____

Check In:

How did you feel once you'd eaten each item?

If you pay attention, your body will tell you when something is and isn't right for you.

_____

_____

Is there anything from today's list that you should get rid of or only eat in moderation?

_____

If so, what?

Are you ready to make these changes? Why or why not?

_____

_____

What did you enjoy the most of all meals?

_____

Instead of giving yourself time limits, give yourself time frames. It'll help you to stop placing limits on yourself and think more about the bigger picture.

Gratitude: What are three things you're grateful for?

_____

_____

Quick Journal: Write one sentence or paragraph of true emotions for the day.

_____

_____

_____

_____

_____

Meditation: Is there anything that you need to release or need clarity on?

_____

Daily Food Tracker:

Day 13:

Breakfast:
_____

Snack:
_____

Lunch:
_____

Snack:
_____

Dinner:
_____

Snack:
_____

Check In:

How did you feel once you'd eaten each item?

If you pay attention, your body will tell you when something is and isn't right for you.

_____

_____

Is there anything from today's list that you should get rid of or only eat in moderation?

_____

If so, what?

Are you ready to make these changes? Why or why not?

_____

_____

What did you enjoy the most of all meals?

_____

Instead of giving yourself time limits, give yourself time frames. It'll help you to stop placing limits on yourself and think more about the bigger picture.

Gratitude: What are three things you're grateful for?

_____

_____

Quick Journal: Write one sentence or paragraph of true emotions for the day.

_____

_____

_____

_____

Meditation: Is there anything that you need to release or need clarity on?
_____

Daily Food Tracker:

Day 14:

Breakfast:
_____

Snack:
_____

Lunch:
_____

Snack:
_____

Dinner:
_____

Snack:
_____

Check In:

How did you feel once you'd eaten each item?

If you pay attention, your body will tell you when something is and isn't right for you.

_____

_____

Is there anything from today's list that you should get rid of or only eat in moderation?

_____

If so, what?

Are you ready to make these changes? Why or why not?

_____

_____

What did you enjoy the most of all meals?

_____

Instead of giving yourself time limits, give yourself time frames. It'll help you to stop placing limits on yourself and think more about the bigger picture.

Gratitude: What are three things you're grateful for?

_____

_____

Quick Journal: Write one sentence or paragraph of true emotions for the day.

_____

_____

_____

_____

Meditation: Is there anything that you need to release or need clarity on?

_____

Daily Food Tracker:

Day 15:

Breakfast:
_____

Snack:
_____

Lunch:
_____

Snack:
_____

Dinner:
_____

Snack:
_____

Check In:

How did you feel once you'd eaten each item?

If you pay attention, your body will tell you when something is and isn't right for you.

_____

_____

Is there anything from today's list that you should get rid of or only eat in moderation?

_____

If so, what?

Are you ready to make these changes? Why or why not?

_____

_____

What did you enjoy the most of all meals?

_____

Instead of giving yourself time limits, give yourself time frames. It'll help you to stop placing limits on yourself and think more about the bigger picture.

Gratitude: What are three things you're grateful for?

_____

_____

Quick Journal: Write one sentence or paragraph of true emotions for the day.

_____

_____

_____

_____

Meditation: Is there anything that you need to release or need clarity on?

_____

Daily Food Tracker:

Day 16:

Breakfast:

_____

Snack:

_____

Lunch:

_____

Snack:

_____

Dinner:

_____

Snack:

_____

Check In:

How did you feel once you'd eaten each item?

If you pay attention, your body will tell you when something is and isn't right for you.

_____

_____

Is there anything from today's list that you should get rid of or only eat in moderation?

_____

If so, what?

Are you ready to make these changes? Why or why not?

_____

_____

What did you enjoy the most of all meals?

_____

Instead of giving yourself time limits, give yourself time frames. It'll help you to stop placing limits on yourself and think more about the bigger picture.

Gratitude: What are three things you're grateful for?

_____

_____

Quick Journal: Write one sentence or paragraph of true emotions for the day.

_____

_____

_____

_____

Meditation: Is there anything that you need to release or need clarity on?

_____

Daily Food Tracker:

Day 17:

Breakfast:

_____

Snack:

_____

Lunch:

_____

Snack:

_____

Dinner:

_____

Snack:

_____

Check In:

How did you feel once you'd eaten each item?

If you pay attention, your body will tell you when something is and isn't right for you.

_____

_____

Is there anything from today's list that you should get rid of or only eat in moderation?

_____

If so, what?

Are you ready to make these changes? Why or why not?

_____

_____

What did you enjoy the most of all meals?

_____

Instead of giving yourself time limits, give yourself time frames. It'll help you to stop placing limits on yourself and think more about the bigger picture.

Gratitude: What are three things you're grateful for?

_____

_____

Quick Journal: Write one sentence or paragraph of true emotions for the day.

_____

_____

_____

_____

Meditation: Is there anything that you need to release or need clarity on?

_____

Daily Food Tracker:

Day 18:

Breakfast:

_____

Snack:

_____

Lunch:

_____

Snack:

_____

Dinner:

_____

Snack:

_____

Check In:

How did you feel once you'd eaten each item?

If you pay attention, your body will tell you when something is and isn't right for you.

_____

_____

Is there anything from today's list that you should get rid of or only eat in moderation?

_____

If so, what?

Are you ready to make these changes? Why or why not?

_____

_____

What did you enjoy the most of all meals?

_____

Instead of giving yourself time limits, give yourself time frames. It'll help you to stop placing limits on yourself and think more about the bigger picture.

Gratitude: What are three things you're grateful for?

_____

_____

Quick Journal: Write one sentence or paragraph of true emotions for the day.

_____

_____

_____

_____

_____

Meditation: Is there anything that you need to release or need clarity on?

_____

Daily Food Tracker:

Day 19:

Breakfast:

_____

Snack:

_____

Lunch:

_____

Snack:

_____

Dinner:

_____

Snack:

_____

Check In:

How did you feel once you'd eaten each item?

If you pay attention, your body will tell you when something is and isn't right for you.

_____

_____

Is there anything from today's list that you should get rid of or only eat in moderation?

_____

If so, what?

Are you ready to make these changes? Why or why not?

_____

_____

What did you enjoy the most of all meals?

_____

Instead of giving yourself time limits, give yourself time frames. It'll help you to stop placing limits on yourself and think more about the bigger picture.

Gratitude: What are three things you're grateful for?

_____

_____

Quick Journal: Write one sentence or paragraph of true emotions for the day.

_____

_____

_____

_____

_____

Meditation: Is there anything that you need to release or need clarity on?

_____

Daily Food Tracker:

Day 20:

Breakfast:
_____

Snack:
_____

Lunch:
_____

Snack:
_____

Dinner:
_____

Snack:
_____

Check In:

How did you feel once you'd eaten each item?

If you pay attention, your body will tell you when something is and isn't right for you.

_____

_____

Is there anything from today's list that you should get rid of or only eat in moderation?

_____

If so, what?

Are you ready to make these changes? Why or why not?

_____

_____

What did you enjoy the most of all meals?

_____

Instead of giving yourself time limits, give yourself time frames. It'll help you to stop placing limits on yourself and think more about the bigger picture.

Gratitude: What are three things you're grateful for?

_____

_____

Quick Journal: Write one sentence or paragraph of true emotions for the day.

_____

_____

_____

_____

Meditation: Is there anything that you need to release or need clarity on?

_____

Daily Food Tracker:

Day 21:

Breakfast:

_____

Snack:

_____

Lunch:

_____

Snack:

_____

Dinner:

_____

Snack:

_____

Check In:

How did you feel once you'd eaten each item?

If you pay attention, your body will tell you when something is and isn't right for you.

_____

_____

Is there anything from today's list that you should get rid of or only eat in moderation?

_____

If so, what?

Are you ready to make these changes? Why or why not?

_____

_____

What did you enjoy the most of all meals?

_____

Instead of giving yourself time limits, give yourself time frames. It'll help you to stop placing limits on yourself and think more about the bigger picture.

Gratitude: What are three things you're grateful for?

_____

_____

Quick Journal: Write one sentence or paragraph of true emotions for the day.

_____

_____

_____

_____

Meditation: Is there anything that you need to release or need clarity on?

_____

Daily Food Tracker:

Day 22:

Breakfast:
_____

Snack:
_____

Lunch:
_____

Snack:
_____

Dinner:
_____

Snack:
_____

Check In:

How did you feel once you'd eaten each item?

If you pay attention, your body will tell you when something is and isn't right for you.

_____

_____

Is there anything from today's list that you should get rid of or only eat in moderation?

_____

If so, what?

Are you ready to make these changes? Why or why not?

_____

_____

What did you enjoy the most of all meals?

_____

Instead of giving yourself time limits, give yourself time frames. It'll help you to stop placing limits on yourself and think more about the bigger picture.

Gratitude: What are three things you're grateful for?

_____
_____

Quick Journal: Write one sentence or paragraph of true emotions for the day.

_____
_____
_____
_____

Meditation: Is there anything that you need to release or need clarity on?

_____

Daily Food Tracker:

Day 23:

Breakfast:
_____

Snack:
_____

Lunch:
_____

Snack:
_____

Dinner:
_____

Snack:
_____

Check In:

How did you feel once you'd eaten each item?

If you pay attention, your body will tell you when something is and isn't right for you.

_____

_____

Is there anything from today's list that you should get rid of or only eat in moderation?

_____

If so, what?

Are you ready to make these changes? Why or why not?

_____

_____

What did you enjoy the most of all meals?

_____

Instead of giving yourself time limits, give yourself time frames. It'll help you to stop placing limits on yourself and think more about the bigger picture.

Gratitude: What are three things you're grateful for?

_____

_____

Quick Journal: Write one sentence or paragraph of true emotions for the day.

_____

_____

_____

_____

_____

Meditation: Is there anything that you need to release or need clarity on?

_____

Daily Food Tracker:

Day 24:

Breakfast:

_____

Snack:

_____

Lunch:

_____

Snack:

_____

Dinner:

_____

Snack:

_____

Check In:

How did you feel once you'd eaten each item?

If you pay attention, your body will tell you when something is and isn't right for you.

_____

_____

Is there anything from today's list that you should get rid of or only eat in moderation?

_____

If so, what?

Are you ready to make these changes? Why or why not?

_____

_____

What did you enjoy the most of all meals?

_____

Instead of giving yourself time limits, give yourself time frames. It'll help you to stop placing limits on yourself and think more about the bigger picture.

Gratitude: What are three things you're grateful for?

_____
_____

Quick Journal: Write one sentence or paragraph of true emotions for the day.

_____
_____
_____
_____
_____

Meditation: Is there anything that you need to release or need clarity on?

_____

Daily Food Tracker:

Day 25:

Breakfast:
_____

Snack:
_____

Lunch:
_____

Snack:
_____

Dinner:
_____

Snack:
_____

Check In:

How did you feel once you'd eaten each item?

If you pay attention, your body will tell you when something is and isn't right for you.

_____

_____

Is there anything from today's list that you should get rid of or only eat in moderation?

_____

If so, what?

Are you ready to make these changes? Why or why not?

_____

_____

What did you enjoy the most of all meals?

_____

Instead of giving yourself time limits, give yourself time frames. It'll help you to stop placing limits on yourself and think more about the bigger picture.

Gratitude: What are three things you're grateful for?

_____

_____

Quick Journal: Write one sentence or paragraph of true emotions for the day.

_____

_____

_____

_____

Meditation: Is there anything that you need to release or need clarity on?

_____

Daily Food Tracker:

Day 26:

Breakfast:

_____

Snack:

_____

Lunch:

_____

Snack:

_____

Dinner:

_____

Snack:

_____

Check In:

How did you feel once you'd eaten each item?

If you pay attention, your body will tell you when something is and isn't right for you.

_____

_____

Is there anything from today's list that you should get rid of or only eat in moderation?

_____

If so, what?

Are you ready to make these changes? Why or why not?

_____

_____

What did you enjoy the most of all meals?

_____

Instead of giving yourself time limits, give yourself time frames. It'll help you to stop placing limits on yourself and think more about the bigger picture.

Gratitude: What are three things you're grateful for?

_____

_____

Quick Journal: Write one sentence or paragraph of true emotions for the day.

_____

_____

_____

_____

_____

Meditation: Is there anything that you need to release or need clarity on?

_____

Daily Food Tracker:

Day 27:

Breakfast:

_____

Snack:

_____

Lunch:

_____

Snack:

_____

Dinner:

_____

Snack:

_____

Check In:

How did you feel once you'd eaten each item?

If you pay attention, your body will tell you when something is and isn't right for you.

_____

_____

Is there anything from today's list that you should get rid of or only eat in moderation?

_____

If so, what?

Are you ready to make these changes? Why or why not?

_____

_____

What did you enjoy the most of all meals?

_____

Instead of giving yourself time limits, give yourself time frames. It'll help you to stop placing limits on yourself and think more about the bigger picture.

Gratitude: What are three things you're grateful for?

_____

_____

Quick Journal: Write one sentence or paragraph of true emotions for the day.

_____

_____

_____

_____

_____

Meditation: Is there anything that you need to release or need clarity on?

_____

Daily Food Tracker:

Day 28:

Breakfast:
_____

Snack:
_____

Lunch:
_____

Snack:
_____

Dinner:
_____

Snack:
_____

Check In:

How did you feel once you'd eaten each item?

If you pay attention, your body will tell you when something is and isn't right for you.

_____

_____

Is there anything from today's list that you should get rid of or only eat in moderation?

_____

If so, what?

Are you ready to make these changes? Why or why not?

_____

_____

What did you enjoy the most of all meals?

_____

Instead of giving yourself time limits, give yourself time frames. It'll help you to stop placing limits on yourself and think more about the bigger picture.

Gratitude: What are three things you're grateful for?

_____

_____

Quick Journal: Write one sentence or paragraph of true emotions for the day.

_____

_____

_____

_____

Meditation: Is there anything that you need to release or need clarity on?

_____

Daily Food Tracker:

Day 29:

Breakfast:

_____

Snack:

_____

Lunch:

_____

Snack:

_____

Dinner:

_____

Snack:

_____

Check In:

How did you feel once you'd eaten each item?

If you pay attention, your body will tell you when something is and isn't right for you.

_____

_____

Is there anything from today's list that you should get rid of or only eat in moderation?

_____

If so, what?

Are you ready to make these changes? Why or why not?

_____

_____

What did you enjoy the most of all meals?

_____

Instead of giving yourself time limits, give yourself time frames. It'll help you to stop placing limits on yourself and think more about the bigger picture.

Gratitude: What are three things you're grateful for?

_____

_____

Quick Journal: Write one sentence or paragraph of true emotions for the day.

_____

_____

_____

_____

Meditation: Is there anything that you need to release or need clarity on?

_____

Daily Food Tracker:

Day 30:

Breakfast:

_____

Snack:

_____

Lunch:

_____

Snack:

_____

Dinner:

_____

Snack:

_____

Check In:

How did you feel once you'd eaten each item?

If you pay attention, your body will tell you when something is and isn't right for you.

_____

_____

Is there anything from today's list that you should get rid of or only eat in moderation?

_____

If so, what?

Are you ready to make these changes? Why or why not?

_____

_____

What did you enjoy the most of all meals?

_____

Instead of giving yourself time limits, give yourself time frames. It'll help you to stop placing limits on yourself and think more about the bigger picture.

KQUALITY QUOTES:

"Allow people to be who they are."
It Doesnt matter who you want them to be, they'll only change and grow if they want to. If you're uncomfortable around them, it's ok to separate from them."

"You're not obligated to share space with anyone who isn't offering peace."

"You can't value time when you're comfortable wasting it."

"The thing about clarity is that it'll lead you to the truth, and sometimes that may be uncomfortable."

"Your actions must speak as beautifully as the words you speak."

"The only way to gain wisdom is to first be a student."

"Let people be nasty on their own."

" If you use others for temporary satisfaction, you will remain internally dissatisfied."

"To judge others, you'd have to assume to be perfect yourself."

"When you're highly committed to your own bullshit, growth sounds more like bullshit than an achievable goal."

"The beauty of her soul really does lie in her eyes."

"Broken people feel entitled to other people's feelings."

"People can't own people, no matter your title. It's not your right to control someone else's feelings."

"People who use others for their temporary satisfaction will remain unhappy."

"When you're highly committed to your own bullshit, growth sounds more like bullshit."

"Nothing amazing grows from stagnancy."

"Your worth is determined by who you've worked to become, not who you're born as.
 "Healthy lifestyles begin with healthy minds."

"Allow yourself to be wanted more than you're needed."

"If your friends and significant other don't support you without great reason, then you should evaluate why you chose them."

"IF THEY HAVE MORE BEAUTY THAN BLUNDER, FOCUS ON THE BEAUTY, ASSIST WITH THE BLUNDER IF YOU'RE MENTALLY ABLE TO."

"IT'S HURTFUL TO LOSE FRIENDS, BUT SOMETIMES YOU OUTGROW YOUR PAST AND OFTEN TIMES THAT INCLUDES FRIENDS."

BEWARE of toxic positivity-This sounds like: don't cry, you're too strong, be happy, it could be worse, at least you don't have to … etc. The issue here is that your feelings are being dismissed because that person isn't comfortable with your truth, so they'd prefer that you'd not talk about it. This is harmful to your growth process. Don't accept it, and don't do it to others.

Weekly/Monthly Goals/Events:

Project(s) to complete:

_____

Time frame: Is there a new baby, graduation, job etc., to prepare for?

_____

Time capsule: Is there a movie, concert, game etc., that you're excited about?

_____

Nature: Does the weather call for sunshine, rain or snow this week/month? Plan some time to enjoy it, whether it's: indoors reading a book, playing a game or soaking up the sun.

_____

Family/Friend: Is there a relative or friend that you can share some time or conversation with? Plan a date night in or out or just a simple text chat about your current status. You can always use a good conversation. Hold nothing back and only share with someone that you trust.

_____

CELEBRATE YOUR SMALL WINS!

Everyone won't celebrate you, and they don't have to. Yes, it feels great to receive support from those who you love, but some people don't know how to celebrate others, and some people just don't want to.

Be mindful of the words that you speak. Words are energy, and when you say or think them, you're allowing them to exist in your space. Make habits of speaking positively often until it becomes your reality.

30 AFFIRMATIONS TO CHOOSE FROM DAILY. RECYCLE WHEN NECESSARY.

1. I AM STRONG ENOUGH TO GET THROUGH THIS DAY!

2. I CAN DO UNBELIEVABLE THINGS!

3. I AM THE LIGHT!

4. I EXUDE POSITIVITY!

5 I GIVE THE LOVE THAT I WANT TO RECEIVE!

6. I AM ENOUGH!

7. I HAVE THE COURAGE TO GROW FROM HERE!

8. I WILL ALLOW MYSELF AND OTHERS GRACE!

9. I FORGIVE THOSE WHO HAVE NEGLECTED ME AND I'LL MOVE FORWARD WITH PEACE

10. I HAVE LIMITLESS POTENTIAL

11. TODAY, I WILL NOT SELF-SABOTAGE

12. I AM ENCOURAGED TO BUILD A PROSPEROUS LIFE

13. I WELCOME ALL CHALLENGES AS A STEPPING STONE TO GREATNESS

14. NOTHING LASTS FOREVER, SO I WONT OWN THE BAD TIMES

15. I NOTICE MY GROWTH AND I'M PROUD OF MYSELF

16. I HAVE THE CONFIDENCE TO STAND TALL FOR MYSELF

17. I OWN MY PEACE !

18. I WILL BE PRESENT IN ALL ASPECTS OF MY LIFE

19. I CAN CHANGE AND GROW

20. MY VISION IS CLEAR AND I WILL PERSEVERE!

21. I HAVE ALL OF THE TOOLS I NEED TO BE MY BEST SELF.

22. I AM FREE OF STRESS

23. I AM CAPABLE OF LOVING FREELY

24. I AM FREE TO LIVE MY BEST LIFE

25. MY MIND AND BODY IS BEAUTIFUL

26. MY HEART IS PURE.

27. TODAY WILL BE A GREAT DAY.

28. I WILL MAKE POSITIVE CONTRIBUTIONS TODAY.

29. I HAVE SELF-CONTROL.

30. LIFE IS BEAUTIFUL

"When you pour from an empty cup, you tend to expect others to replace it."

"To find the beauty in others, you must first find it within." ~ Quali

Find something beautiful within today.

Make time to smell the fresh air and If you pass a rose, stop and appreciate the beauty.

"To understand your placement in life, you have to value your worth."

"Though the truth may seem less pretty, be fearless in owning yours."

Be Dope!

WHAT IS SOMETHING FROM YOUR PAST THAT YOU NEED TO COMPLETELY LET GO OF BUT HAVEN'T BECAUSE IT'S UNCOMFORTABLE TO ADDRESS? (SUCH AS PAIN, LOSS OR FAILURE.)

*NOTE: LETTING GO MEANS THAT IT NO LONGER HOLDS YOU MENTALLY HOSTAGE, AND IT'S NO LONGER UNCOMFORTABLE OR HURTFUL.

SUPPRESSING YOUR EMOTIONS CAN HAVE YOU FEELING LIKE YOU'VE ACTUALLY MOVED ON, BUT ALL YOU'VE DONE IS NORMALIZE YOUR DYSFUNCTIONAL SIDE EFFECTS.

BE HONEST ABOUT HOW IT MAKES YOU FEEL AND WHY IT MAKES YOU FEEL THAT WAY. TAKE SOME REAL TIME TO WORK OUT THE DETAILS.
NO MORE HIDING. NO MORE SUFFOCATING.

_____
_____
_____
_____
_____
_____
_____
_____
_____
_____
_____
_____
_____
_____
_____
_____
_____
_____
_____
_____
_____
_____
_____
_____
_____
_____
_____
_____
_____
_____
_____

DESTINATION HAPPY

There is no destination, vacation, person, or thing that's going to offer you permanent happiness. It's been said a time or a dozen that happiness is an inside job. It's been kept as a surface-level explanation and often causes confusion.

Some will look at the lives of others and want to emulate them without knowing or caring what it took to get there or if said person is even actually happy.

Happiness begins with an understanding of what it means to you.

What does happiness mean to you?
_____
_____

What does a happy life look like to you?
_____
_____

What do you want in this life?
_____
_____

How close are you to having the life that you desire?
_____
_____

What's holding you back from having the life that you want?
_____
_____

What work have you done to get to your desired stage of happiness?
_____
_____

Why is this important to you?
_____
_____

Joy vs. happy

Happy is an emotion. It's momentary.
Joy is internal, it's a light within. When you're not having the best moments, it'll soon pass because the joy that you carry will remind you that everything can and will get better.

Imagine your greater self and lifestyle. What does this look like?

Create your new lifestyle. Let your imagination flow. There's no wrong answer.
Whatever your answers may be, there's truth in it. You can have this new life and more if you truly believe it and put forth the efforts to make it happen.
You got this!

_____

_____

_____

_____

_____

_____

_____

_____

_____

_____

_____

_____

_____

There's so much to explore in a life full of mystery.

What's the worst that can happen from you taking risks?

___

___

___

___

___

___

___

What's the best that could happen from you taking risks?

___

___

___

___

RESPECT:

What is your definition of respect?
_____
_____

How important is respect to you?
_____
_____

How well do you respect yourself by your definition?
_____
_____

How often do you allow others to disrespect you?
_____
_____

Are you respectful of others?
_____
_____

Respect is defined as holding someone in high regards. When you respect yourself, it sets the standard for how others see you and should treat you.

If fear had a mirror, what would the reflection look like?

What are your greatest fears?

_____

_____

Is this fear something that could actually happen?

_____

_____

How often has it happened to someone that you know personally?

_____

_____

Fear is crippling.

It can keep you from trying new things and is often times the culprit for unhappiness.

Whatever your fears are, whether big or small, educate yourself on them.

Learn why you're so triggered by them and work on how to let go of fear.

You're surrounded by beauty; take some time to sit and enjoy it.

LOVE:

It's something that we all need, and many desire just to have it.

Oftentimes, people will create illusions of what love looks like and spend more time focused on the image and less time on the connection.

What does your perfect love look and feel like?
_____
_____

What's your ultimate love goal?
_____
_____

What have you done to achieve this goal?
_____

Great! Now that you know what you want, are you willing to make changes and/or efforts to receive the love that you desire?

If yes, then you first have to accept the love within you.
Once you can love yourself properly, you're then able to give and receive love wholeheartedly.

SELF-LOVE: Self-love has less to do with self-admiration and is more about your desire for inner peace. When you choose inner peace, you'll make any change necessary to involve only the things that fuel you and rid all else.

You can admire yourself, but if your insides are ugly, you won't have much to desire.

Self-love is an inside job that takes real time and dedication. If you could have the best organic relationships, would you be willing to work for it?

How much time have you given to loving yourself?

This is not to be confused with pampering and grooming. Though it may feel good, it's just aesthetics, which will eventually fade.

When you're invested in self-love, it doesn't fade. Every day may not be the best, but once your foundation is solid, you can always get back to happy days.

Only you know what work needs to be done or undone.

Do your daily task sheets. Answer the questions honestly, without self-judgment. Your truth is yours alone, and if you're unhappy with it, there's time and space for change and growth.

Once you understand yourself better, you'll unravel all that you need to let go of and accept it.

Self-love is the greatest love of all.

Allow those who choose to love you in.

Don't waste time forcing those who choose not to—this is where broken hearts lie.

Healing broken hearts.

A great way to cause pain to yourself is to expect others to be someone they're not.

You're doing yourself and others a great disservice by placing them on pedestals. No one is above being a human being, and no one can match up to a storybook character

Mental Health Check-in:

What is your current mood?
_____

If not good, what are you doing to change things?
_____

How has your mood been lately?
_____

Your mood doesn't have to be great every day or all day each day, because you are human, but if you notice that's it's mostly bad, there's a chance that you're not in control of your emotions — whether its due to mental or medical health issues, you can get help.

Actions that can be taken:
o Meditation for clarity and understanding
o Therapy for assistance with understanding
o Confront the issue after you have a clear understanding and start the work to grow. Keep an open mind and heart.

Are you in an environment that affects your daily functionality? (This could be work or home.)
_____

Do you need to leave the space that you reside in? (This could be work or home.)
_____

Do you feel safe?
_____

Mental Health Check-in:

What is your current mood?
_____

If not good, what are you doing to change things?
_____

How has your mood been lately?
_____

Your mood doesn't have to be great every day or all day each day, because you are human, but if you notice that's it's mostly bad, there's a chance that you're not in control of your emotions — whether it's due to mental or medical health issues, you can get help.

Actions that can be taken:
o Meditation for clarity and understanding
o Therapy for assistance with understanding
o Confront the issue after you have a clear understanding and start the work to grow. Keep an open mind and heart.

Are you in an environment that affects your daily functionality? (This could be work or home.)
_____

Do you need to leave the space that you reside in? (This could be work or home.)
_____

Do you feel safe?
_____

Mental Health Check-in:

What is your current mood?
_____

If not good, what are you doing to change things?
_____

How has your mood been lately?
_____

Your mood doesn't have to be great every day or all day each day, because you are human, but if you notice that's it's mostly bad, there's a chance that you're not in control of your emotions, but you can always work on that.

Actions that can be taken:
o Meditation for clarity and understanding
o Therapy for assistance with understanding
o Confront the issue after you have a clear understanding and start the work to grow. Keep an open mind and heart.

Are you in an environment that affects your daily functionality? (This could be work or home.)
_____

Do you need to leave the space that you reside in? (This could be work or home.)
_____

Do you feel safe?
_____

Mental Health Check-in:

What is your current mood?
_____

If not good, what are you doing to change things?
_____

How has your mood been lately?
_____

Your mood doesn't have to be great every day or all day each day, because you are human, but if you notice that's it's mostly bad, there's a chance that you're not in control of your emotions, but you can always work on that.

Actions that can be taken:
- Meditation for clarity and understanding
- Therapy for assistance with understanding
- Confront the issue after you have a clear understanding and start the work to grow. Keep an open mind and heart.

Are you in an environment that affects your daily functionality? (This could be work or home.)
_____

Do you need to leave the space that you reside in? (This could be work or home.)
_____

Do you feel safe?
_____

Mental Health Check-in:

What is your current mood?
_____

If not good, what are you doing to change things?
_____

How has your mood been lately?
_____

Your mood doesn't have to be great every day or all day each day, because you are human, but if you notice that's it's mostly bad, there's a chance that you're not in control of your emotions — whether it's due to mental or medical health issues, you can get help.

Actions that can be taken:
- Meditation for clarity and understanding
- Therapy for assistance with understanding
- Confront the issue after you have a clear understanding and start the work to grow. Keep an open mind and heart.

Are you in an environment that affects your daily functionality? (This could be work or home.)
_____

Do you need to leave the space that you reside in? (This could be work or home.)
_____

Do you feel safe?
_____

Mental Health Check-in:

What is your current mood?
_____

If not good, what are you doing to change things?
_____

How has your mood been lately?
_____

Your mood doesn't have to be great every day or all day each day, because you are human, but if you notice that's it's mostly bad, there's a chance that you're not in control of your emotions — whether it's due to mental or medical health issues, you can get help.

Actions that can be taken:
- Meditation for clarity and understanding
- Therapy for assistance with understanding
- Confront the issue after you have a clear understanding and start the work to grow. Keep an open mind and heart.

Are you in an environment that affects your daily functionality? (This could be work or home.)
_____

Do you need to leave the space that you reside in? (This could be work or home.)
_____

Do you feel safe?
_____

Mental Health Check-in:

What is your current mood?
_____

If not good, what are you doing to change things?
_____

How has your mood been lately?
_____

Your mood doesn't have to be great every day or all day each day, because you are human, but if you notice that's it's mostly bad, there's a chance that you're not in control of your emotions — whether it's due to mental or medical health issues, you can get help.

Actions that can be taken:
o Meditation for clarity and understanding
o Therapy for assistance with understanding
o Confront the issue after you have a clear understanding and start the work to grow. Keep an open mind and heart.

Are you in an environment that affects your daily functionality? (This could be work or home.)
_____

Do you need to leave the space that you reside in? (This could be work or home.)
_____

Do you feel safe?
_____

Mental Health Check-in:

What is your current mood?
_____

If not good, what are you doing to change things?
_____

How has your mood been lately?
_____

Your mood doesn't have to be great every day or all day each day, because you are human, but if you notice that's it's mostly bad, there's a chance that you're not in control of your emotions — whether it's due to mental or medical health issues, you can get help.

Actions that can be taken:
- Meditation for clarity and understanding
- Therapy for assistance with understanding
- Confront the issue after you have a clear understanding and start the work to grow. Keep an open mind and heart.

Are you in an environment that affects your daily functionality? (This could be work or home.)
_____

Do you need to leave the space that you reside in? (This could be work or home.)
_____

Do you feel safe?
_____

Mental Health Check-in:

What is your current mood?
_____

If not good, what are you doing to change things?
_____

How has your mood been lately?
_____

Your mood doesn't have to be great every day or all day each day, because you are human, but if you notice that's it's mostly bad, there's a chance that you're not in control of your emotions — whether it's due to mental or medical health issues, you can get help.

Actions that can be taken:
o Meditation for clarity and understanding
o Therapy for assistance with understanding
o Confront the issue after you have a clear understanding and start the work to grow. Keep an open mind and heart.

Are you in an environment that affects your daily functionality? (This could be work or home.)
_____

Do you need to leave the space that you reside in? (This could be work or home.)
_____

Do you feel safe?
_____

Mental Health Check-in:

What is your current mood?
_____

If not good, what are you doing to change things?
_____

How has your mood been lately?
_____

Your mood doesn't have to be great every day or all day each day, because you are human, but if you notice that's it's mostly bad, there's a chance that you're not in control of your emotions — — whether it's due to mental or medical health issues, you can get help.

Actions that can be taken:
- Meditation for clarity and understanding
- Therapy for assistance with understanding
- Confront the issue after you have a clear understanding and start the work to grow. Keep an open mind and heart.

Are you in an environment that affects your daily functionality? (This could be work or home.)
_____

Do you need to leave the space that you reside in? (This could be work or home.)
_____

Do you feel safe?
_____

Mental Health Check-in:

What is your current mood?
_____

If not good, what are you doing to change things?
_____

How has your mood been lately?
_____

Your mood doesn't have to be great every day or all day each day, because you are human, but if you notice that's it's mostly bad, there's a chance that you're not in control of your emotions — — whether it's due to mental or medical health issues, you can get help.

Actions that can be taken:
- Meditation for clarity and understanding
- Therapy for assistance with understanding
- Confront the issue after you have a clear understanding and start the work to grow. Keep an open mind and heart.

Are you in an environment that affects your daily functionality? (This could be work or home.)
_____

Do you need to leave the space that you reside in? (This could be work or home.)
_____

Do you feel safe?
_____

Mental Health Check-in:

What is your current mood?
_____

If not good, what are you doing to change things?
_____

How has your mood been lately?
_____

Your mood doesn't have to be great every day or all day each day, because you are human, but if you notice that's it's mostly bad, there's a chance that you're not in control of your emotions — — whether it's due to mental or medical health issues, you can get help.

Actions that can be taken:
o Meditation for clarity and understanding
o Therapy for assistance with understanding
o Confront the issue after you have a clear understanding and start the work to grow. Keep an open mind and heart.

Are you in an environment that affects your daily functionality? (This could be work or home.)
_____

Do you need to leave the space that you reside in? (This could be work or home.)
_____

Do you feel safe?
_____

Mental Health Check-in:

What is your current mood?
_____

If not good, what are you doing to change things?
_____

How has your mood been lately?
_____

Your mood doesn't have to be great every day or all day each day, because you are human, but if you notice that's it's mostly bad, there's a chance that you're not in control of your emotions — — whether it's due to mental or medical health issues, you can get help.

Actions that can be taken:
o Meditation for clarity and understanding
o Therapy for assistance with understanding
o Confront the issue after you have a clear understanding and start the work to grow. Keep an open mind and heart.

Are you in an environment that affects your daily functionality? (This could be work or home.)
_____

Do you need to leave the space that you reside in? (This could be work or home.)
_____

Do you feel safe?
_____

Mental Health Check-in:

What is your current mood?
_____

If not good, what are you doing to change things?
_____

How has your mood been lately?
_____

Your mood doesn't have to be great every day or all day each day, because you are human, but if you notice that's it's mostly bad, there's a chance that you're not in control of your emotions — — whether it's due to mental or medical health issues, you can get help.

Actions that can be taken:
o Meditation for clarity and understanding
o Therapy for assistance with understanding
o Confront the issue after you have a clear understanding and start the work to grow. Keep an open mind and heart.

Are you in an environment that affects your daily functionality? (This could be work or home.)
_____

Do you need to leave the space that you reside in? (This could be work or home.)
_____

Do you feel safe?
_____

Mental Health Check-in:

What is your current mood?
_____

If not good, what are you doing to change things?
_____

How has your mood been lately?
_____

Your mood doesn't have to be great every day or all day each day, because you are human, but if you notice that's it's mostly bad, there's a chance that you're not in control of your emotions — — whether it's due to mental or medical health issues, you can get help.

Actions that can be taken:
- Meditation for clarity and understanding
- Therapy for assistance with understanding
- Confront the issue after you have a clear understanding and start the work to grow. Keep an open mind and heart.

Are you in an environment that affects your daily functionality? (This could be work or home.)
_____

Do you need to leave the space that you reside in? (This could be work or home.)
_____

Do you feel safe?
_____

Mental Health Check-in:

What is your current mood?
_____

If not good, what are you doing to change things?
_____

How has your mood been lately?
_____

Your mood doesn't have to be great every day or all day each day, because you are human, but if you notice that's it's mostly bad, there's a chance that you're not in control of your emotions — — whether it's due to mental or medical health issues, you can get help.

Actions that can be taken:
o Meditation for clarity and understanding
o Therapy for assistance with understanding
o Confront the issue after you have a clear understanding and start the work to grow. Keep an open mind and heart.

Are you in an environment that affects your daily functionality? (This could be work or home.)
_____

Do you need to leave the space that you reside in? (This could be work or home.)
_____

Do you feel safe?
_____

Mental Health Check-in:

What is your current mood?
_____

If not good, what are you doing to change things?
_____

How has your mood been lately?
_____

Your mood doesn't have to be great every day or all day each day, because you are human, but if you notice that's it's mostly bad, there's a chance that you're not in control of your emotions — — whether it's due to mental or medical health issues, you can get help.

Actions that can be taken:
o Meditation for clarity and understanding
o Therapy for assistance with understanding
o Confront the issue after you have a clear understanding and start the work to grow. Keep an open mind and heart.

Are you in an environment that affects your daily functionality? (This could be work or home.)
_____

Do you need to leave the space that you reside in? (This could be work or home.)
_____

Do you feel safe?
_____

Mental Health Check-in:

What is your current mood?
_____

If not good, what are you doing to change things?
_____

How has your mood been lately?
_____

Your mood doesn't have to be great every day or all day each day, because you are human, but if you notice that's it's mostly bad, there's a chance that you're not in control of your emotions — — whether it's due to mental or medical health issues, you can get help.

Actions that can be taken:
o Meditation for clarity and understanding
o Therapy for assistance with understanding
o Confront the issue after you have a clear understanding and start the work to grow. Keep an open mind and heart.

Are you in an environment that affects your daily functionality? (This could be work or home.)
_____

Do you need to leave the space that you reside in? (This could be work or home.)
_____

Do you feel safe?
_____

Mental Health Check-in:

What is your current mood?
_____

If not good, what are you doing to change things?
_____

How has your mood been lately?
_____

Your mood doesn't have to be great every day or all day each day, because you are human, but if you notice that's it's mostly bad, there's a chance that you're not in control of your emotions — — whether it's due to mental or medical health issues, you can get help.

Actions that can be taken:
- Meditation for clarity and understanding
- Therapy for assistance with understanding
- Confront the issue after you have a clear understanding and start the work to grow. Keep an open mind and heart.

Are you in an environment that affects your daily functionality? (This could be work or home.)
_____

Do you need to leave the space that you reside in? (This could be work or home.)
_____

Do you feel safe?
_____

Mental Health Check-in:

What is your current mood?
_____

If not good, what are you doing to change things?
_____

How has your mood been lately?
_____

Your mood doesn't have to be great every day or all day each day, because you are human, but if you notice that's it's mostly bad, there's a chance that you're not in control of your emotions — — whether it's due to mental or medical health issues, you can get help.

Actions that can be taken:
o Meditation for clarity and understanding
o Therapy for assistance with understanding
o Confront the issue after you have a clear understanding and start the work to grow. Keep an open mind and heart.

Are you in an environment that affects your daily functionality? (This could be work or home.)
_____

Do you need to leave the space that you reside in? (This could be work or home.)
_____

Do you feel safe?
_____

Mental Health Check-in:

What is your current mood?
_____

If not good, what are you doing to change things?
_____

How has your mood been lately?
_____

Your mood doesn't have to be great every day or all day each day, because you are human, but if you notice that's it's mostly bad, there's a chance that you're not in control of your emotions — — whether it's due to mental or medical health issues, you can get help.

Actions that can be taken:
o Meditation for clarity and understanding
o Therapy for assistance with understanding
o Confront the issue after you have a clear understanding and start the work to grow. Keep an open mind and heart.

Are you in an environment that affects your daily functionality? (This could be work or home.)
_____

Do you need to leave the space that you reside in? (This could be work or home.)
_____

Do you feel safe?
_____

Mental Health Check-in:

What is your current mood?
_____

If not good, what are you doing to change things?
_____

How has your mood been lately?
_____

Your mood doesn't have to be great every day or all day each day, because you are human, but if you notice that's it's mostly bad, there's a chance that you're not in control of your emotions — — whether it's due to mental or medical health issues, you can get help.

Actions that can be taken:
o Meditation for clarity and understanding
o Therapy for assistance with understanding
o Confront the issue after you have a clear understanding and start the work to grow. Keep an open mind and heart.

Are you in an environment that affects your daily functionality? (This could be work or home.)
_____

Do you need to leave the space that you reside in? (This could be work or home.)
_____

Do you feel safe?
_____

Mental Health Check-in:

What is your current mood?
_____

If not good, what are you doing to change things?
_____

How has your mood been lately?
_____

Your mood doesn't have to be great every day or all day each day, because you are human, but if you notice that's it's mostly bad, there's a chance that you're not in control of your emotions — — whether it's due to mental or medical health issues, you can get help.

Actions that can be taken:
o Meditation for clarity and understanding
o Therapy for assistance with understanding
o Confront the issue after you have a clear understanding and start the work to grow. Keep an open mind and heart.

Are you in an environment that affects your daily functionality? (This could be work or home.)
_____

Do you need to leave the space that you reside in? (This could be work or home.)
_____

Do you feel safe?
_____

Mental Health Check-in:

What is your current mood?
_____

If not good, what are you doing to change things?
_____

How has your mood been lately?
_____

Your mood doesn't have to be great every day or all day each day, because you are human, but if you notice that's it's mostly bad, there's a chance that you're not in control of your emotions — — whether it's due to mental or medical health issues, you can get help.

Actions that can be taken:
o Meditation for clarity and understanding
o Therapy for assistance with understanding
o Confront the issue after you have a clear understanding and start the work to grow. Keep an open mind and heart.

Are you in an environment that affects your daily functionality? (This could be work or home.)
_____

Do you need to leave the space that you reside in? (This could be work or home.)
_____

Do you feel safe?
_____

Mental Health Check-in:

What is your current mood?
_____

If not good, what are you doing to change things?
_____

How has your mood been lately?
_____

Your mood doesn't have to be great every day or all day each day, because you are human, but if you notice that's it's mostly bad, there's a chance that you're not in control of your emotions — — whether it's due to mental or medical health issues, you can get help.

Actions that can be taken:
o Meditation for clarity and understanding
o Therapy for assistance with understanding
o Confront the issue after you have a clear understanding and start the work to grow. Keep an open mind and heart.

Are you in an environment that affects your daily functionality? (This could be work or home.)
_____

Do you need to leave the space that you reside in? (This could be work or home.)
_____

Do you feel safe?
_____

Mental Health Check-in:

What is your current mood?
_____

If not good, what are you doing to change things?
_____

How has your mood been lately?
_____

Your mood doesn't have to be great every day or all day each day, because you are human, but if you notice that's it's mostly bad, there's a chance that you're not in control of your emotions — — whether it's due to mental or medical health issues, you can get help.

Actions that can be taken:
o Meditation for clarity and understanding
o Therapy for assistance with understanding
o Confront the issue after you have a clear understanding and start the work to grow. Keep an open mind and heart.

Are you in an environment that affects your daily functionality? (This could be work or home.)
_____

Do you need to leave the space that you reside in? (This could be work or home.)
_____

Do you feel safe?
_____

Mental Health Check-in:

What is your current mood?
_____

If not good, what are you doing to change things?
_____

How has your mood been lately?
_____

Your mood doesn't have to be great every day or all day each day, because you are human, but if you notice that's it's mostly bad, there's a chance that you're not in control of your emotions — — whether it's due to mental or medical health issues, you can get help.

Actions that can be taken:
o Meditation for clarity and understanding
o Therapy for assistance with understanding
o Confront the issue after you have a clear understanding and start the work to grow. Keep an open mind and heart.

Are you in an environment that affects your daily functionality? (This could be work or home.)
_____

Do you need to leave the space that you reside in? (This could be work or home.)
_____

Do you feel safe?
_____

Mental Health Check-in:

What is your current mood?
_____

If not good, what are you doing to change things?
_____

How has your mood been lately?
_____

Your mood doesn't have to be great every day or all day each day, because you are human, but if you notice that's it's mostly bad, there's a chance that you're not in control of your emotions — — whether it's due to mental or medical health issues, you can get help.

Actions that can be taken:
- Meditation for clarity and understanding
- Therapy for assistance with understanding
- Confront the issue after you have a clear understanding and start the work to grow. Keep an open mind and heart.

Are you in an environment that affects your daily functionality? (This could be work or home.)
_____

Do you need to leave the space that you reside in? (This could be work or home.)
_____

Do you feel safe?
_____

Mental Health Check-in:

What is your current mood?
_____

If not good, what are you doing to change things?
_____

How has your mood been lately?
_____

Your mood doesn't have to be great every day or all day each day, because you are human, but if you notice that's it's mostly bad, there's a chance that you're not in control of your emotions — — whether it's due to mental or medical health issues, you can get help.

Actions that can be taken:
o Meditation for clarity and understanding
o Therapy for assistance with understanding
o Confront the issue after you have a clear understanding and start the work to grow. Keep an open mind and heart.

Are you in an environment that affects your daily functionality? (This could be work or home.)
_____

Do you need to leave the space that you reside in? (This could be work or home.)
_____

Do you feel safe?
_____

Mental Health Check-in:

What is your current mood?
_____

If not good, what are you doing to change things?
_____

How has your mood been lately?
_____

Your mood doesn't have to be great every day or all day each day, because you are human, but if you notice that's it's mostly bad, there's a chance that you're not in control of your emotions — — whether it's due to mental or medical health issues, you can get help.

Actions that can be taken:
- Meditation for clarity and understanding
- Therapy for assistance with understanding
- Confront the issue after you have a clear understanding and start the work to grow. Keep an open mind and heart.

Are you in an environment that affects your daily functionality? (This could be work or home.)
_____

Do you need to leave the space that you reside in? (This could be work or home.)
_____

Do you feel safe?
_____

Mental Health Check-in:

What is your current mood?
_____

If not good, what are you doing to change things?
_____

How has your mood been lately?
_____

Your mood doesn't have to be great every day or all day each day, because you are human, but if you notice that's it's mostly bad, there's a chance that you're not in control of your emotions —
— whether it's due to mental or medical health issues, you can get help.

Actions that can be taken:
- Meditation for clarity and understanding
- Therapy for assistance with understanding
- Confront the issue after you have a clear understanding and start the work to grow. Keep an open mind and heart.

Are you in an environment that affects your daily functionality? (This could be work or home.)
_____

Do you need to leave the space that you reside in? (This could be work or home.)
_____

Do you feel safe?
_____

Energy Level Checker

Is your energy being used wisely?

Yes or No

Are you giving time and effort to people and things that fuel you or things that are depleting you?

A) I only make time for all things that fuel me.

or

B) I'm still a work in progress, and sometimes I'm depleted from the people and things that I choose to give my energy to.

Once you're aware of how important reserving as much of your healthy energy for yourself is, you'll become uncomfortable and/or irritable around anyone or thing that's draining.

MO MONEY = MO PROBLEMS OR LESS MONEY = MO PROBLEMS?

Money is such a taboo subject that should be discussed more. It's something that we all need to survive and there are unfortunately so many people with poor money management.

It's been reported that most Americans go into debt by age 25, including student loans and credit cards. I'm not sure about you, but I was just starting to live real life at that age and I'm uncomfortable knowing that before I can get an adult job, I'm forced to have adult bills.

Instead of dwelling on the things that I cannot/couldn't change, I look for ways to get ahead. Gratefully, there's a lot of educational resources.

What does your financial blueprint look like?
_____

Do you make enough money to pay your bills and save or are you living above your means?
_____

If you're only making enough money to pay bills or barely covering the bills then you have to make some financial changes.

Think about how this can work for you.

Some options are: Add more streams of income, work over time at your current job, or simply stop spending on frivolous things especially if those things can't make you more money.

 Only you can know exactly how much you can take on, but you must know that freeing yourself from a dysfunctional money blueprint can relieve lots of stress and unnecessary spending. Understand that bills will always be a factor so get in front of it before you get behind.

_____

Is there an asset that you want to invest in, specific cars that you want to own, businesses that you want to create, vacations that you want to take? Etc. Write everything down that comes to mind.

___

How close are you to having these things?

1) I'm almost there

2) Not even close

3) I need more time and education

Kindness is the quality of being generous and considerate — doing something because you want to, not because you feel like you're obligated to or that you deserve reciprocity.

What is the kindest thing you've done for yourself this year?

_____

_____

_____

What is the kindest thing you've done for another person this year?

_____

_____

_____

It's amazing to do nice things for others, as you should be of service to others and to yourself, but make time to care about your days as much as you do for others.
Pouring from a half-empty glass can lead to burnout quickly, and if you can't give 100 percent of yourself, then why even do it?

What does the best version of yourself look like?

Mentally _____

_____

_____

Physically _____

_____

_____

Spiritually _____

_____

_____

Are you really willing to make the efforts to become this person?

_____

What are you willing to let go of in order to become this person?

_____

_____

Letting go of anyone or anything that no longer serves a purpose can be difficult, but very rewarding.
Normalizing dysfunction just to keep some familiarity can be more damaging for your mental health as well as physical.

Think about the one thing or person that really isn't good for you, but you refuse to let go because of how comfortable you've become having it/them around.
Think about how it /they holds you back from reaching your goals.

Don't mistake longevity for love.
Time doesn't equate to love. The work that's put in to make the love last is what counts.

"Relationships can have expiration dates. Get out before it's spoiled."

Ignorance

Greed

Selfishness

Fear

Human Nature

Love

Lust

Hate

Emotions

Hope

Courage

KEEP YOUR FOOT ON YOUR OWN NECK FIRST.

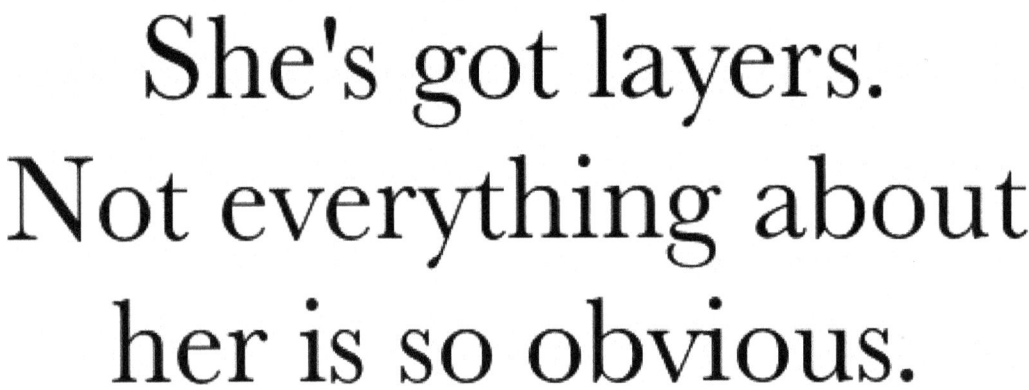

She's got layers.
Not everything about
her is so obvious.

Be selfish with yourself until they're worth all of you.

Personal Mission Statement:

A mission statement helps to determine your values by sharing your ultimate goal and how you'll accomplish them.

Set concrete goals, be honest about the things that you need to complete, make a list and check them off accordingly.

Short-term goals: these can be daily, weekly, or annually.

What is your short-term goal, and what do you plan to do to accomplish this goal?

Long-term goals: something to accomplish In the future.

The amount of time is determined by you but make sure they're realistic and that your short-term goals are helping you achieve long-term goals.

Example:

Long-term goal: in three years, I want to be a traveling yoga instructor with clientele in three states.

Short-term goal: I want to practice yoga at least three times a week, meditate daily for at least ten mins, eat less junk food and more healthy meals that are made for my body, practice mindfulness and positivity.

(I'm practicing everyday so that I can become certified in three months. I'll then travel to teach while building a clientele.)

My mission statement: become a healthier version of myself mentally, physically, and spiritually so that I can help others do the same.

Happy Life:

What does this mean to you? If you could control how your life would be, what would this look like?

Starting from childhood, Describe your happy life:

_____

_____

_____

_____

_____

_____

_____

_____

_____

_____

_____

_____

_____

Healing:

What is something from your past that you need to let go of but are afraid to address?

Example: pain, loss, failure.

Start with the most important one first, write it down and address it.

Unravel the truth by learning to understand why it's so bothersome to you.

Imagine your greater self and lifestyle. What does this look like?
Create your new lifestyle. Let your imagination flow. There's no wrong answer.

    Whatever your answers may be, there's truth in it. You can have this new life and more if you truly believe it and put forth the efforts to make it happen.
You got this!

_____

_____

_____

_____

_____

_____

_____

_____

_____

_____

_____

CHECK IN! DON'T ALLOW YOURSELF TO DROWN.